Breaking Free: How to Overcome Anxiety and Depression

1. --
2. Summary
3. Chapter 2
4. Chapter 1: Understanding Anxiety and Depression
5. Chapter 2: The Global Impact of Anxiety and Depression
6. Chapter 3: Personal Stories of Struggle and Triumph
7. Chapter 4: Foundations of Managing Symptoms
8. Chapter 5: Cognitive-Behavioral Techniques for Healing
9. Chapter 6: Embracing Mindfulness and Meditation
10. Chapter 7: Expert Opinions on Therapeutic Approaches
11. Chapter 8: Customizable Tools for Individual Needs
12. Chapter 9: Empirical Evidence and Empathetic Storytelling
13. Chapter 10: Reflective Exercises for Self-Discovery
14. Chapter 11: Navigating Complexities with Confidence
15. Chapter 12: A Pathway Illuminated by Compassion and Practical Wisdom
16. Synopsis

Summary

Chapter 1: Understanding Anxiety and Depression	3
1.1 The Nature of Anxiety: Beyond the Basics	3
1.2 Depression Unveiled: More Than Just Sadness	5
1.3 Physiological, Psychological, and Social Dimensions	7
Chapter 2: The Global Impact of Anxiety and Depression	9
2.1 Prevalence and Statistics Worldwide	9
2.2 The Societal Cost: From Productivity to Personal Relationships	1:
2.3 The Economic Burden of Mental Health	1:
Chapter 3: Personal Stories of Struggle and Triumph	1:
3.1 Voices from the Darkness: Real-Life Experiences	1:
3.2 Paths to Healing: Diverse Journeys Toward Recovery	1'
3.3 Finding Hope in the Darkest Moments	1!
Chapter 4: Foundations of Managing Symptoms	2
4.1 Recognizing Triggers and Patterns	2
4.2 Building a Support System: Family, Friends, and Professionals	2:
4.3 Creating a Safe Space for Healing	2:
Chapter 5: Cognitive-Behavioral Techniques for Healing	2'
5.1 Understanding Cognitive Distortions	2'
5.2 Implementing Behavioral Changes	2!
5.3 Challenging Negative Thought Patterns	3
Chapter 6: Embracing Mindfulness and Meditation	3:
6.1 Introduction to Mindfulness Practices	3:
6.2 Step-by-Step Guide to Meditation	3:
6.3 Cultivating Self-Awareness through Mindfulness	3'

Chapter 7: Expert Opinions on Therapeutic Approaches
7.1 Insights from Clinical Experience
7.2 Research Excellence in Mental Health Treatments
7.3 The Role of Medication in Treatment Plans
Chapter 8: Customizable Tools for Individual Needs
8.1 Adapting Strategies for Personal Circumstances
8.2 Creating Your Mental Health Toolkit
8.3 Prioritizing Self-Care in Daily Life
Chapter 9: Empirical Evidence and Empathetic Storytelling
9.1 Bridging Science with Human Experience
9.2 Engaging Readers in a Transformative Process
9.3 The Power of Vulnerability in Healing
Chapter 10: Reflective Exercises for Self-Discovery
10.1 Encouraging Active Engagement with Content
10.2 Fostering Agency in the Healing Journey
10.3 Uncovering Personal Strengths and Resilience
Chapter 11: Navigating Complexities with Confidence
11.1 Overcoming Obstacles in Mental Health Challenges
11.2 Strategies for Sustaining Progress
11.3 Building Resilience in the Face of Adversity
Chapter 12: A Pathway Illuminated by Compassion and Practical Wisdom
12.1 Supporting Others in Their Battle Against Anxiety and Depression
12.2 Conclusion: Reclaiming Control Over Mental Well-being
12.3 Embracing a Brighter Future with Hope and Confidence

1 Understanding Anxiety and Depression

1.1 The Nature of Anxiety: Beyond the Basics

Anxiety, often perceived merely as a common reaction to stress, holds a much more complex and profound significance in the realm of mental health. Its nature extends beyond the occasional worry or fear, embedding itself deeply into an individual's daily functioning and quality of life. Understanding anxiety on this deeper level is crucial for those seeking to overcome its grip.

The physiological underpinnings of anxiety reveal a sophisticated interplay between the brain's neural pathways and hormonal responses. When confronted with perceived threats, the body's fight-or-flight mechanism is activated, releasing a cascade of stress hormones like cortisol and adrenaline. While this response is designed to protect us in moments of danger, in individuals with anxiety disorders, this system can become overly responsive, leading to persistent feelings of unease even in the absence of actual threats.

Psychologically, anxiety can manifest through a range of symptoms from excessive worrying and difficulty concentrating to more severe manifestations such as panic attacks. These experiences are not only distressing but can also interfere significantly with personal relationships, academic performance, and professional achievements. The cognitive aspect of anxiety involves constant rumination and anticipation of future disasters, which further entrenches the cycle of fear and avoidance behaviors.

Socially, anxiety has far-reaching implications that extend beyond the individual sufferer. It can strain relationships with family members, friends, and colleagues due to misunderstandings about the condition's legitimacy and its impact on social interactions. Moreover, societal stigma surrounding mental health issues often discourages people from seeking help or discussing their struggles openly.

In recent years, research has begun to shed light on novel therapeutic approaches aimed at addressing these multifaceted aspects of anxiety. Innovations in treatment now emphasize not only traditional psychotherapy and medication but also incorporate mindfulness practices, lifestyle modifications, and digital interventions designed to empower individuals with tools for managing their symptoms.

By delving into these dimensions—physiological responses, psychological impacts, social consequences—and exploring emerging treatments beyond conventional methods, we gain a comprehensive understanding of anxiety's true nature. This holistic perspective is essential for anyone looking to navigate their way through the complexities of anxiety disorders towards a path of recovery.

1.2 Depression Unveiled: More Than Just Sadness

Depression, often misconstrued as merely a profound sense of sadness, unfolds into a complex psychological state that transcends the occasional blues. Its unveiling in this discussion aims to broaden the understanding of depression as a multifaceted disorder that impacts every aspect of an individual's life. Far from being just about feeling sad, depression encompasses a range of symptoms that can severely impair one's ability to function and enjoy life.

The misconception of depression as simple sadness belies its true complexity. It is a condition characterized by persistent feelings of despair, worthlessness, and disinterest in activities once found pleasurable. Unlike typical mood fluctuations, depression affects how a person thinks, feels, and handles daily activities for an extended period. This distinction is crucial for recognizing the seriousness of the disorder and the necessity for comprehensive treatment approaches.

Physiologically, depression has been linked to alterations in brain chemistry and structure. Research indicates that imbalances in neurotransmitters like serotonin, dopamine, and norepinephrine play a significant role in its development. Moreover, neuroimaging studies have shown changes in areas of the brain responsible for mood regulation, cognitive function, and decision-making among those with depression. These findings underscore the biological underpinnings of depression, challenging the stigma that it is simply a matter of willpower or mindset.

Psychologically and emotionally, individuals with depression often experience a pervasive sense of hopelessness and an inability to derive pleasure from activities they once enjoyed—a condition known as anhedonia. The depth of emotional pain can lead to existential despair and thoughts of self-harm or suicide. Cognitive symptoms such as difficulty concentrating, remembering details, or making decisions further exacerbate feelings of inadequacy and worthlessness.

Socially, depression can be isolating. The withdrawal from social interactions—often due to fatigue or feelings of being a burden—can strain relationships with family members and friends. This isolation creates a vicious cycle that can worsen depressive symptoms by reinforcing feelings of loneliness and disconnection.

In conclusion, understanding depression requires acknowledging its complexity beyond mere sadness. It is imperative to recognize its physiological causes, psychological manifestations, and social implications to foster empathy towards those affected and promote effective interventions. By delving into these aspects with sensitivity and depth, we pave the way for more nuanced discussions about mental health challenges.

1.3 Physiological, Psychological, and Social Dimensions of Anxiety and Depression

The exploration of anxiety and depression reveals a complex interplay between physiological, psychological, and social dimensions that collectively influence the manifestation and experience of these mental health conditions. Understanding these dimensions is crucial for developing effective treatment strategies and providing comprehensive support to those affected.

Physiological Aspects: Anxiety and depression are not merely emotional states but are deeply rooted in biological processes. Research has shown that genetic predisposition plays a significant role in the risk of developing these conditions. Neurobiological factors, including imbalances in neurotransmitters such as serotonin, dopamine, and norepinephrine, contribute to the symptoms of anxiety and depression. These chemical messengers are essential for regulating mood, sleep, appetite, and cognition. Furthermore, chronic stress can lead to alterations in the hypothalamic-pituitary-adrenal (HPA) axis, exacerbating the physiological response to stress and potentially leading to or worsening anxiety and depression.

Psychological Dimensions: The psychological impact of anxiety and depression encompasses a wide range of cognitive and emotional symptoms. Individuals may experience persistent worry or fear in the case of anxiety or feelings of sadness, hopelessness, and loss of interest in previously enjoyed activities in the case of depression. Cognitive distortions such as pessimistic thinking patterns, overgeneralization, and catastrophizing can aggravate these conditions by perpetuating negative thought cycles. Moreover, psychological theories suggest that early life experiences, coping mechanisms developed over time, personality traits such as neuroticism, and cognitive appraisal processes significantly influence one's vulnerability to anxiety and depression.

Social Factors: The social dimension plays a pivotal role in both the onset and progression of anxiety and depression. Social isolation, lack of supportive relationships, experiences of bullying or abuse, socioeconomic status challenges, cultural factors affecting stigma around mental health—all contribute to an individual's risk profile for developing these disorders. Additionally, how society perceives mental health issues can affect an individual's willingness to seek help due to fear of judgment or discrimination.

In conclusion, *the intricate relationship between physiological processes, psychological resilience, and social environments* underscores the complexity of anxiety and depression. Addressing only one aspect may provide limited relief; hence a holistic approach considering all three dimensions is essential for effective management and recovery from these debilitating conditions.

The Global Impact of Anxiety and Depressi[on]

2.1 Prevalence and Statistics Worldwide

The global landscape of mental health, particularly concerning anxiety and depression, presents a complex and challenging picture. The prevalence of these conditions underscores a pressing public health issue that transcends geographical, cultural, and socio-economic boundaries. With nearly 264 million individuals affected by depression globally, as highlighted in recent statistics, the scale of this challenge is immense. Furthermore, the intersectionality with anxiety disorders, affecting approximately 40% of those with depression, amplifies the urgency for comprehensive understanding and action.

This widespread prevalence is not just a number; it represents millions of lives intertwined with the struggles associated with these mental health conditions. The impact is profound, affecting individuals' daily functioning, relationships, productivity, and overall quality of life. Moreover, the societal implications are significant, encompassing increased healthcare costs, reduced workforce participation, and heightened social isolation.

Delving deeper into the statistics reveals disparities in prevalence rates across different regions and demographics. For instance, high-income countries report higher diagnosed instances of both anxiety and depression compared to low- and middle-income countries. This discrepancy may reflect differences in diagnostic practices, access to healthcare services, or varying levels of stigma associated with mental health issues. Additionally, gender plays a crucial role in the prevalence rates of these conditions; women are nearly twice as likely as men to suffer from anxiety and depression.

The age at which individuals are most vulnerable to these conditions also provides critical insights into their pervasive nature. While anxiety disorders frequently manifest during adolescence or early adulthood setting a trajectory for lifelong challenges if left unaddressed—depression shows a broader age range at onset but peaks among adults aged 25 to 44 years old.

Understanding these statistics is vital for framing global mental health strategies that are inclusive and effective. It highlights the need for targeted interventions that consider demographic-specific vulnerabilities while promoting universal access to mental health care services. As we navigate through this data-driven landscape of anxiety and depression prevalence worldwide, it becomes increasingly clear that addressing these conditions requires concerted efforts from all sectors of society.

2.2 The Societal Cost: From Productivity to Personal Relationships

The societal impact of anxiety and depression extends far beyond the individual, affecting every facet of society from economic productivity to the fabric of personal relationships. These mental health conditions not only diminish the quality of life for millions but also impose a heavy burden on global economies and social structures.

At the heart of this issue is the significant reduction in workforce productivity. Anxiety and depression often lead to absenteeism, where individuals find themselves unable to attend work due to their symptoms. Equally concerning is presenteeism, a scenario in which employees are physically present at their workplace but operate at reduced capacity because of their mental health state. This dual threat to productivity can result in substantial financial losses for businesses and economies, with estimates running into billions annually worldwide.

Beyond the economic implications, anxiety and depression deeply affect personal relationships and social cohesion. Individuals suffering from these conditions may experience difficulties in maintaining healthy relationships, leading to increased isolation and sometimes even contributing to family breakdowns. The strain placed on personal connections can create a cycle of social withdrawal and loneliness, exacerbating the mental health issues at hand.

The healthcare system itself faces challenges due to the high demand for mental health services, which often outstrips supply. This imbalance can lead to long waiting times for treatment, during which individuals' conditions may deteriorate further. Moreover, there is a significant economic cost associated with providing care for those affected by anxiety and depression, including direct costs like therapy sessions and medication, as well as indirect costs such as lost productivity.

In addressing these societal costs, it's crucial to consider preventive measures and early intervention strategies that can mitigate the impact of anxiety and depression. Promoting mental health awareness in workplaces, schools, and within families can play a key role in early detection and support. Additionally, enhancing access to mental health services ensures timely treatment for those in need, potentially reducing long-term societal costs.

Ultimately, understanding the full scope of societal costs associated with anxiety and depression underscores the importance of collective action in tackling these pervasive conditions. By fostering supportive environments both at work and home while investing in robust mental health services, societies can begin to alleviate the profound impact these disorders have on individuals' lives and overall societal well-being.

2.3 The Economic Burden of Mental Health

The economic implications of mental health, particularly anxiety and depression, are profound and multifaceted, impacting not just the global economy but also the financial stability of individual households. This section delves into the various dimensions through which mental health disorders exert their economic toll, highlighting both direct and indirect costs that contribute to the overall burden on society.

Direct costs associated with mental health care include expenses for psychiatric hospitalizations, outpatient visits, medications, and therapy sessions. These are often compounded by the high out-of-pocket expenses for patients and their families, which can lead to significant financial strain. In many countries, inadequate insurance coverage for mental health services exacerbates this issue, limiting access to necessary care and resulting in uneven distribution of healthcare resources.

Indirect costs, while less visible, are equally impactful. They encompass lost productivity due to absenteeism—where individuals cannot attend work because of their mental health condition—and presenteeism—where employees are at work but operating at reduced capacity. The ripple effects extend into decreased employment opportunities and lower income levels for those affected by severe mental health issues. Moreover, there is a substantial impact on caregivers who may have to reduce their working hours or exit the workforce entirely to provide support, further straining household finances.

The broader economic landscape is also affected through reduced consumer spending and increased dependency on social welfare systems. Long-term unemployment or underemployment among those with chronic anxiety or depression contributes to a cycle of poverty and social exclusion that can be challenging to break. Additionally, businesses face increased insurance premiums and additional costs related to employee turnover and retraining.

In conclusion, understanding the full scope of the economic burden imposed by mental health conditions underscores the need for concerted efforts across sectors to address this challenge. By prioritizing mental health as a key component of public health policy and ensuring equitable access to care, societies can alleviate not only the personal but also the economic impacts of these conditions.

To mitigate these economic burdens, investment in comprehensive mental health services is crucial. Early intervention programs can reduce the severity of symptoms and improve long-term outcomes for individuals with anxiety or depression. Workplaces adopting mental health initiatives can see a return on investment through increased productivity and reduced healthcare costs. Furthermore, enhancing public awareness about mental health can help reduce stigma, encouraging more people to seek treatment early.

3 Personal Stories of Struggle and Triump

3.1 Voices from the Darkness: Real-Life Experiences

In the shadowy realms of mental health, where anxiety and depression lurk, real-life stories emerge as powerful beacons of insight. These narratives, drawn from the depths of personal struggle, illuminate the complex interplay between mental illness and the human spirit's resilience. "Voices from the Darkness" delves into these experiences, offering a raw and unfiltered glimpse into the lives of individuals who have navigated through their darkest hours.

The significance of sharing these stories cannot be overstated. They serve not only as a testament to individual endurance but also as a source of hope for others facing similar battles. Each account is unique, reflecting the diverse ways in which anxiety and depression can manifest and affect lives. From young adults grappling with the pressures of academia to professionals overwhelmed by stress and isolation, these stories span a broad spectrum of experiences.

One narrative might describe a college student's struggle with social anxiety, detailing how it hampered their ability to engage in everyday activities and pursue opportunities. Another could recount a veteran's battle with PTSD and depression following their return from service, highlighting the challenges of reintegration into civilian life. Through these personal accounts, readers gain an intimate understanding of the internal conflicts that characterize these conditions.

The transformative power of therapy and support networks in facilitating recovery.

The role of self-care practices in managing symptoms and improving quality of life.

The importance of breaking down stigma and fostering open conversations about mental health.

Moreover, "Voices from the Darkness" emphasizes that while anxiety and depression are formidable foes, they are not insurmountable. It showcases various coping mechanisms individuals have adopted—ranging from professional treatment like therapy and medication to personal strategies such as mindfulness meditation, exercise, or creative expression. These stories underscore that healing is possible and that no one is alone in their journey.

Ultimately, this section aims to connect readers with real-world examples that resonate on a deeply personal level. By presenting an array of perspectives on overcoming anxiety and depression, it encourages empathy, understanding, and solidarity among those affected by these conditions. In doing so, "Voices from the Darkness" contributes significantly to demystifying mental illness and promoting a more compassionate society.

3.2 Paths to Healing: Diverse Journeys Toward Recovery

The journey toward recovery from mental health challenges is as unique as the individuals who embark on it. While "Voices from the Darkness" provides a window into the personal struggles with anxiety and depression, this section delves into the myriad paths people take towards healing and recovery. Understanding these diverse journeys is crucial in recognizing that there is no one-size-fits-all solution to mental health issues, and what works for one person may not work for another.

One of the most significant steps on this journey is often acknowledging the need for help, which can be a formidable hurdle due to stigma or self-denial. Once this barrier is crossed, individuals find themselves exploring various therapeutic options. Traditional psychotherapy remains a cornerstone of treatment, offering a safe space for individuals to process their emotions and experiences under the guidance of a professional. Cognitive Behavioral Therapy (CBT), in particular, has shown effectiveness in treating anxiety and depression by challenging negative thought patterns.

Medication can also play a critical role in managing symptoms for some, acting as a tool that enables further exploration of underlying issues through therapy or other means. However, it's important to note that medication affects everyone differently, and finding the right type and dosage can be a process of trial and error.

Beyond conventional treatments, many have found solace in alternative therapies such as mindfulness meditation, yoga, or art therapy. These practices offer different ways of connecting with oneself and can be particularly appealing to those seeking holistic approaches to wellness.

Support networks form another essential element of recovery. Whether it's friends and family offering understanding and encouragement or support groups providing empathy from those with similar experiences, feeling connected can significantly impact an individual's healing process.

Finally, lifestyle changes encompassing diet, exercise, sleep hygiene, and stress management have been recognized for their positive effects on mental health. For many individuals dealing with anxiety and depression, integrating these habits into daily life has been transformative.

In conclusion, paths to healing are varied and complex. They reflect the multifaceted nature of mental health itself—interwoven with physical well-being, emotional resilience, social connections, and personal growth. By embracing this diversity in journeys toward recovery, we open up a spectrum of possibilities for healing tailored to each individual's needs.

3.3 Finding Hope in the Darkest Moments

The essence of finding hope in the darkest moments lies not just in the search for light but in recognizing that even in the deepest shadows, growth and understanding can emerge. This journey is deeply personal and varies greatly from one individual to another, reflecting the unique ways people navigate through their struggles towards a semblance of peace or resolution.

At the heart of these stories are moments of realization—epiphanies where individuals understand that their pain, however overwhelming, does not define their entirety. It's a profound acknowledgment that while darkness may be a part of their life, it is not the whole. Such realizations often come unexpectedly: during a conversation, while engaging in art or music, or even in solitude amidst nature's tranquility.

Therapeutic interventions play a crucial role in many recovery narratives. For some, traditional therapy sessions provide a structured environment where emotions and thoughts can be unpacked with professional guidance. Others find solace in more holistic approaches like mindfulness practices or physical activities which reconnect them with their bodies and the present moment. These methods do not serve as universal solutions but are significant steps on diverse paths toward healing.

Equally important is the power of connection—finding hope through relationships with others who have faced similar battles. Support groups and communities offer spaces where experiences are shared without judgment, fostering an environment of mutual understanding and empathy. Here, individuals are reminded they are not alone; their feelings are valid, and their experiences resonate with others.

Lifestyle adjustments also contribute significantly to this journey. Incorporating routines that promote physical well-being—such as regular exercise, nutritious diets, and adequate sleep—can enhance mental health by improving mood and reducing anxiety levels. Moreover, engaging in hobbies or interests provides distractions from distressing thoughts and channels energy into productive and fulfilling activities.

In conclusion, finding hope in the darkest moments is about discovering light within oneself—a light that persists despite external circumstances. It's about building resilience through self-compassion, connections with others, therapeutic practices, and lifestyle changes that nurture both body and mind.

Each story of struggle is unique; yet each carries a universal message about the human capacity to seek out hope amidst despair.

4 Foundations of Managing Symptoms

4.1 Recognizing Triggers and Patterns

Understanding the intricacies of anxiety and depression involves more than just identifying symptoms; it requires a deep dive into recognizing triggers and patterns that exacerbate these conditions. This knowledge is pivotal in managing mental health effectively, as it empowers individuals to anticipate and mitigate the impact of potential stressors. Triggers can be as varied as personal relationships, work-related stress, financial worries, or even changes in weather. Similarly, patterns of behavior or thought that precede episodes of anxiety or depression can offer critical insights into how these conditions manifest uniquely in each individual.

Recognizing triggers and patterns is not an intuitive process for everyone. It often necessitates a period of reflection and observation, sometimes guided by mental health professionals. Journaling daily activities, emotions, and reactions can serve as a practical tool in this discovery process. By documenting their experiences consistently, individuals may begin to notice correlations between specific events or thoughts and their mental state. This self-awareness is the first step towards developing personalized coping strategies.

Moreover, understanding triggers and patterns extends beyond personal benefit. It also enhances the support system around the person affected by anxiety or depression. Friends, family members, and caregivers who are aware of these triggers and patterns can avoid unintentional exacerbation of symptoms and provide more effective support during challenging times.

In addition to self-observation and journaling, professional help plays a crucial role in identifying triggers and patterns accurately. Therapists trained in cognitive-behavioral techniques can help individuals recognize negative thought patterns that contribute to their anxiety or depression. Through therapy sessions, people learn to challenge these thoughts and replace them with healthier alternatives.

Ultimately, recognizing triggers and patterns is about gaining control over one's mental health journey. It allows for proactive management of symptoms through avoidance of known triggers when possible or preparation for their impact when they cannot be avoided. This approach fosters resilience by equipping individuals with the knowledge to navigate their condition more effectively.

4.2 Building a Support System: Family, Friends, and Professionals

The journey of managing symptoms related to mental health conditions like anxiety and depression is significantly influenced by the support system surrounding an individual. Building a robust network of family, friends, and professionals is not just beneficial but essential for effective symptom management. This network serves as a multifaceted resource that provides emotional support, practical assistance, and professional guidance.

Family members and friends play a crucial role in the support system. They offer love, understanding, and a sense of belonging that can be incredibly comforting during difficult times. However, their involvement goes beyond emotional support. Educating loved ones about the nature of mental health conditions helps them recognize signs of distress and understand the importance of triggers and patterns identified in earlier stages. This knowledge enables them to contribute positively to the individual's coping strategies rather than inadvertently exacerbating symptoms.

Professional support complements the care provided by family and friends by offering specialized knowledge and treatment options tailored to the individual's needs. Mental health professionals such as therapists, psychologists, and psychiatrists can diagnose conditions accurately, recommend appropriate therapies or medications, and provide ongoing monitoring of progress. Their expertise is invaluable in developing effective management plans that address both immediate symptoms and long-term wellness goals.

In addition to traditional therapy sessions, support groups—either in-person or online—offer another layer of professional guidance mixed with peer support. These groups create safe spaces where individuals can share experiences, strategies for coping with symptoms, and encouragement from others who truly understand what it means to live with anxiety or depression.

Building this comprehensive support system requires openness from the individual seeking help as well as willingness from family, friends, and professionals to engage actively in their recovery process. It's a collaborative effort that emphasizes communication, education, and mutual respect across all parties involved.

Ultimately, establishing a strong foundation of support not only aids in managing current symptoms but also empowers individuals to navigate future challenges more effectively. It fosters resilience by ensuring that people do not have to face their struggles alone but have a network ready to stand beside them every step of the way.

4.3 Creating a Safe Space for Healing

The concept of creating a safe space for healing is pivotal in the journey towards managing and overcoming symptoms of mental health conditions.

This environment, both physical and emotional, serves as a sanctuary where individuals feel secure to express themselves, explore their feelings, and engage in therapeutic activities without fear of judgment or harm. The creation of such spaces is integral to fostering resilience and promoting recovery.

A safe healing space is characterized by its ability to offer comfort and support while respecting the individual's boundaries and needs. It is a place where trust is built between the person seeking help and those providing care, whether they are family members, friends, or professionals. In this environment, open communication is encouraged, allowing individuals to share their experiences and challenges freely.

Physical aspects of a safe space can vary widely depending on personal preferences but often include settings that are quiet, private, and filled with natural light or soothing colors. Comfortable seating, access to nature or greenery, and the absence of clutter can also contribute to creating a calming atmosphere that facilitates relaxation and introspection.

Emotionally, a safe healing space requires an understanding from those within it that mental health struggles are complex and multifaceted. Empathy, patience, and unconditional positive regard are key components in nurturing an environment where individuals feel valued and understood. It's important for caregivers and support networks to actively listen without offering unsolicited advice or minimizing the person's feelings.

In addition to family support, professional environments such as therapy offices or group meeting spaces should also embody these principles of safety. Mental health professionals play a crucial role in establishing these environments through their approach to treatment. Techniques may include setting clear boundaries at the outset of therapy, ensuring confidentiality, and adopting an empathetic listening stance that fosters mutual respect.

Ultimately, creating a safe space for healing is about more than just physical surroundings; it's about cultivating an atmosphere where individuals battling mental health conditions can embark on their recovery journey with confidence. By prioritizing safety in both tangible and intangible ways, we empower those struggling with mental health issues to reclaim control over their lives in an environment that champions their well-being above all else.

Cognitive-Behavioral Techniques for Healing

5.1 Understanding Cognitive Distortions

Cognitive distortions are at the heart of how we perceive stress, challenges, and our abilities to overcome them. These skewed perceptions can significantly impact our mental health, contributing to anxiety and depression. Understanding these distortions is crucial for anyone looking to break free from the cycle of negative thinking that often accompanies these conditions. By identifying and challenging our distorted thoughts, we can begin to see situations more clearly and respond to them in a healthier way.

Cognitive distortions come in many forms, each distorting our view of reality in unique ways. For instance, 'black-and-white thinking' leads us to see everything in extremes—something is either perfect or a total failure with no middle ground. Another common distortion is 'catastrophizing,' where we expect the worst possible outcome in any situation, often leading to significant anxiety about events that may never happen.

Other distortions include 'overgeneralization,' where we take one instance and generalize it to every aspect of life; 'jumping to conclusions,' where we interpret things negatively without evidence; and 'personalization,' where we blame ourselves for every bad thing that happens, regardless of our actual involvement. Each of these distortions can contribute to a cycle of negative thinking that feeds into anxiety and depression.

To combat cognitive distortions, it's essential first to become aware of them. This awareness allows us to question and challenge these automatic thoughts instead of accepting them as truth. Techniques such as cognitive-behavioral therapy (CBT) are particularly effective in this regard, offering structured ways to identify and dispute irrational thoughts. By practicing these techniques regularly, individuals can gradually change their patterns of thinking, leading to improved mental health outcomes.

Black-and-White Thinking

Catastrophizing

Overgeneralization

Jumping to Conclusions

Personalization

In conclusion, understanding cognitive distortions is a vital step towards overcoming anxiety and depression. By learning how these distortions shape our perception of reality, we empower ourselves with the tools needed not only to challenge negative thought patterns but also to build a more positive outlook on life.

5.2 Implementing Behavioral Changes

The journey from understanding cognitive distortions to implementing behavioral changes is a critical transition in cognitive-behavioral therapy (CBT). Recognizing and challenging distorted thoughts is an essential first step, but the ultimate goal is to translate this newfound awareness into tangible actions that promote healthier mental habits. This phase is where the theoretical knowledge of CBT becomes practical, allowing individuals to actively reshape their behaviors in ways that support their mental health.

Implementing behavioral changes requires a structured approach, often beginning with small, manageable adjustments that gradually build up to more significant lifestyle alterations. The rationale behind starting small lies in the concept of self-efficacy; achieving minor goals can boost confidence and motivation, making larger goals seem more attainable. For instance, someone struggling with social anxiety might start by initiating brief conversations with acquaintances before progressing to attending larger social gatherings.

Behavioral activation is a common technique used in this stage, encouraging individuals to engage in activities they find enjoyable or fulfilling. This method counters patterns of avoidance and withdrawal that often accompany depression and anxiety. By systematically increasing their level of activity, individuals can disrupt the cycle of negative thoughts and feelings that perpetuate these conditions.

Another crucial aspect of implementing behavioral changes involves developing coping strategies for dealing with stress and triggers. These strategies might include relaxation techniques such as deep breathing or progressive muscle relaxation, as well as problem-solving skills to navigate challenging situations more effectively. The key is for individuals to have a toolkit of responses at their disposal, rather than relying on maladaptive behaviors like substance abuse or withdrawal.

Goal setting plays a pivotal role throughout this process. Effective goals are specific, measurable, achievable, relevant, and time-bound (SMART). Setting SMART goals helps ensure that objectives are clear and realistic, providing a roadmap for change that can be adjusted as needed based on progress and feedback.

In conclusion, implementing behavioral changes is a dynamic process that builds on the foundation laid by understanding cognitive distortions. It involves taking proactive steps towards altering behaviors in meaningful ways, supported by techniques such as behavioral activation and effective coping strategies. Through consistent practice and perseverance, these changes can significantly improve mental health outcomes.

5.3 Challenging Negative Thought Patterns

The journey of cognitive-behavioral therapy (CBT) progresses from recognizing cognitive distortions to actively challenging and altering negative thought patterns. This critical phase is pivotal for individuals seeking to break free from the cycle of negative thinking that exacerbates mental health issues like anxiety and depression. Challenging these patterns is not merely about disputing negative thoughts but involves a comprehensive strategy to reframe and replace them with more balanced, realistic perspectives.

One foundational technique in this process is the identification of automatic negative thoughts (ANTs). These are the instinctive responses or thoughts that often skew towards negativity, arising from underlying beliefs about oneself, others, or the world. By learning to catch these ANTs in the moment, individuals can begin the work of questioning their validity and utility. Questions such as "Is this thought based on facts or my interpretation?" or "Does this thought help me achieve my goals?" can be instrumental in this self-interrogation process.

Another crucial aspect involves understanding the link between thoughts, emotions, and behaviors. This triad suggests that our thoughts influence our feelings, which in turn affect our actions. By changing how we think, we can alter how we feel and behave in any given situation. Techniques such as cognitive restructuring aim to dismantle the distorted thinking patterns by examining evidence for and against particular thoughts, thus encouraging a more balanced view.

Mindfulness practices play a significant role in challenging negative thought patterns by fostering an attitude of non-judgmental awareness. Through mindfulness, individuals learn to observe their thoughts without immediately reacting to them emotionally.

Journaling is another effective tool that allows for tracking thoughts over time, providing tangible evidence of progress and areas needing further work.

Behavioral experiments challenge negative predictions by testing them out in real-world scenarios, thereby offering direct evidence against some of the catastrophic outcomes anticipated by negative thinking.

In conclusion, challenging negative thought patterns requires a multifaceted approach that combines awareness with active questioning and behavioral strategies. It's a skill developed over time through consistent practice but offers profound benefits including reduced anxiety and depression symptoms, improved mood regulation, and greater overall mental resilience. As individuals learn to navigate their internal landscapes with more compassion and less judgment, they unlock new pathways towards healing and well-being.

6 Embracing Mindfulness and Meditation

6.1 Introduction to Mindfulness Practices

In the contemporary landscape of mental health, mindfulness practices emerge as a vital tool for alleviating the symptoms of anxiety and depression, conditions affecting millions globally. This section delves into the essence of mindfulness, its historical roots, and its application in modern therapeutic contexts. By understanding mindfulness at its core, individuals can embark on a journey towards greater mental well-being, equipped with practices that foster a sense of peace, presence, and self-compassion.

Mindfulness is fundamentally about being fully present in the moment, aware of where we are and what we're doing, without becoming overly reactive or overwhelmed by what's going on around us. Though it has origins in Buddhist meditation practices, mindfulness has transcended cultural and religious boundaries to become a universally embraced approach for enhancing mental health. The practice encourages an attitude of openness and curiosity towards one's experiences, promoting a compassionate engagement with one's thoughts and feelings.

The relevance of mindfulness in addressing anxiety and depression cannot be overstated. These conditions often involve excessive rumination on past events or worries about the future. Mindfulness counters this tendency by anchoring individuals in the present moment, thereby disrupting patterns of negative thought that fuel emotional distress. Research supports its efficacy; numerous studies have documented how regular mindfulness practice can significantly reduce symptoms of anxiety and depression, improve mood, and increase overall quality of life.

Implementing mindfulness into daily life doesn't necessitate extensive periods of meditation; rather, it can be integrated through simple exercises such as mindful breathing, walking meditation, or even mindful eating. These practices do not require special equipment or considerable time investment but do demand consistency and intentionality. By cultivating an awareness of the breath or engaging fully with the sensory experience of walking or eating, individuals learn to observe their thoughts and feelings without judgment or immediate reaction.

Moreover, mindfulness fosters resilience against future stressors. As individuals become more adept at noticing their internal experiences without becoming entangled in them, they develop a stronger foundation from which to face challenges with equanimity. This aspect is particularly crucial for those dealing with anxiety and depression since it equips them with tools to manage potential triggers more effectively.

In conclusion, embracing mindfulness practices offers a pathway towards healing for those afflicted by anxiety and depression. By learning to inhabit the present moment with kindness towards oneself and one's experiences, individuals can unlock profound levels of inner peace and emotional stability. As this chapter unfolds further strategies will be explored but beginning this journey with an understanding of mindfulness lays down essential groundwork for overcoming mental health challenges.

6.2 Step-by-Step Guide to Meditation

Meditation, a cornerstone of mindfulness practice, offers profound benefits for mental health, particularly in managing anxiety and depression. This guide provides a structured approach to meditation, designed to help individuals cultivate a deeper sense of presence and peace. By breaking down the process into manageable steps, this guide aims to make meditation accessible to everyone, regardless of experience level.

The first step in beginning a meditation practice is finding a quiet space where you can be undisturbed for the duration of your session. This doesn't require a special room or equipment; a comfortable chair or cushion in a peaceful corner of your home will suffice. The key is consistency, so try to use the same space each time you meditate.

Once you have found your space, set aside a specific time each day for meditation. Starting with just five minutes daily can be effective, gradually increasing the duration as you become more comfortable with the practice. Consistency is crucial; meditating at the same time each day helps establish it as a habit.

Begin your meditation by adopting a comfortable seated position with your back straight but not rigid. This posture helps maintain alertness throughout your session. Close your eyes or lower your gaze to reduce visual distractions.

The next step involves focusing on your breath. Notice the sensation of air entering and leaving your nostrils or the rise and fall of your chest as you breathe naturally. Your breath serves as an anchor to the present moment, helping to quieten the mind.

When thoughts arise—and they will—gently acknowledge them without judgment and return your focus to your breath.

If sitting still becomes uncomfortable, incorporate gentle movements such as mindful walking into your practice.

End each session by slowly opening your eyes and taking a moment to notice how you feel before getting up gradually.

Incorporating mindfulness techniques such as body scans or loving-kindness meditations can further enrich your practice over time. A body scan involves paying attention to different parts of the body in turn, noting any sensations without judgment. Loving-kindness meditation focuses on cultivating feelings of goodwill towards oneself and others.

Meditation is not about achieving perfection but practicing patience and kindness towards oneself throughout the journey. Regular practice cultivates an awareness that extends beyond formal sessions into everyday life, enhancing one's ability to remain present and reducing susceptibility to anxiety and depression.

In conclusion, this step-by-step guide offers an accessible pathway for integrating meditation into daily life. By fostering greater mindfulness through regular practice, individuals can unlock profound levels of inner peace and emotional stability, contributing significantly to their mental well-being.

6.3 Cultivating Self-Awareness through Mindfulness

Mindfulness, at its core, is the practice of becoming more aware of our thoughts, emotions, and sensations in the present moment without judgment. This heightened state of awareness is a powerful tool for cultivating self-awareness, a critical component in understanding ourselves better and navigating life's challenges with greater ease. By integrating mindfulness into our daily routines, we can develop a deeper connection with our inner selves, leading to enhanced emotional intelligence and resilience.

The journey towards cultivating self-awareness through mindfulness begins with simple practices that focus on the breath and body. These practices ground us in the present moment and serve as the foundation for observing our internal experiences. As we become more adept at noticing our thoughts and feelings without getting caught up in them, we start to recognize patterns in our reactions and behaviors. This recognition is the first step towards self-understanding.

One effective method for enhancing self-awareness is mindful meditation. This involves sitting quietly and paying attention to the breath, bodily sensations, or even sounds around us. When distractions arise, as they inevitably will, we gently acknowledge them and return our focus to the object of meditation. Over time, this practice helps us develop a non-reactive stance towards our thoughts and emotions, allowing us to observe them more objectively.

Engaging in regular body scans can further deepen self-awareness by bringing attention to physical sensations throughout the body. This not only promotes relaxation but also helps identify areas where we might be holding stress or tension.

Practicing mindful walking integrates movement with awareness, offering an opportunity to observe how our bodies feel in motion while staying connected to the environment around us.

Incorporating mindfulness into everyday activities like eating or listening can transform routine actions into moments of deep presence and connection.

Beyond individual practices, maintaining a journal can be an invaluable tool for reflecting on experiences observed through mindfulness. Writing about thoughts and emotions as they arise provides insights into personal habits and thought patterns, fostering a greater understanding of oneself.

Cultivating self-awareness through mindfulness is not an overnight process but rather a lifelong journey that unfolds gradually with patience and persistence. As we become more attuned to our inner world, we gain clarity about who we are and what matters most to us. This clarity empowers us to make choices that align with our true selves, leading to a more fulfilling life.

In conclusion, embracing mindfulness as a pathway to self-awareness offers profound benefits for personal growth and well-being. By dedicating time each day to mindful practices, we open ourselves up to discovering deeper truths about who we are and how we relate to the world around us.

Expert Opinions on Therapeutic Approach

7.1 Insights from Clinical Experience

The journey to overcoming anxiety and depression is deeply personal, yet universally challenging. Insights from clinical experience shed light on the nuanced understanding that mental health professionals have developed through years of treating patients with these conditions. This depth of knowledge offers a unique perspective on therapeutic approaches, emphasizing the importance of individualized treatment plans.

Clinical experience underscores the complexity of anxiety and depression, revealing that these are not monolithic entities but rather spectrums of disorders with varying symptoms, triggers, and effective treatments. Therapists and psychiatrists often draw upon a rich tapestry of strategies to address the multifaceted nature of these conditions. From cognitive-behavioral therapy (CBT) to medication, mindfulness practices, and lifestyle changes, the arsenal available is vast and varied.

One key insight from clinical practice is the critical role of a strong therapeutic alliance between patient and therapist. This relationship serves as the foundation for effective treatment, providing the trust and safety necessary for patients to explore difficult emotions, challenge distorted thinking patterns, and experiment with new behaviors. Clinicians emphasize that healing is not linear; it involves setbacks and breakthroughs alike. Therefore, patience, persistence, and adaptability are crucial qualities that both therapists and patients must cultivate.

Personalization of treatment plans stands out as a cornerstone of successful therapy. Clinicians often combine different modalities based on the patient's specific needs, preferences, history, and response to previous treatments.

Engagement in therapy is significantly enhanced when patients actively participate in setting their treatment goals and selecting therapeutic activities.

Mindfulness-based interventions have gained prominence for their effectiveness in increasing awareness of present-moment experiences, thereby reducing symptoms of anxiety and depression.

In conclusion, insights from clinical experience contribute invaluable guidance for navigating the complexities of treating anxiety and depression. These perspectives highlight the importance of a tailored approach that considers each individual's unique journey towards mental wellness. By integrating empirical evidence with compassionate care, clinicians play an instrumental role in helping individuals break free from the shackles of anxiety and depression.

7.2 Research Excellence in Mental Health Treatments

The pursuit of excellence in research on mental health treatments is a dynamic and evolving field, driven by the imperative to understand and effectively address the complex nature of mental disorders. This section delves into the cutting-edge methodologies, innovative treatment modalities, and interdisciplinary collaborations that are setting new standards in the care and recovery of individuals with mental health conditions.

At the forefront of this exploration is the integration of technology into therapeutic practices. Digital interventions, such as online cognitive-behavioral therapy (CBT) platforms and mobile applications for mood tracking, have revolutionized access to mental health resources, enabling personalized care at scale. These technologies not only extend the reach of traditional therapies but also offer new insights into patient engagement and treatment efficacy through data analytics.

Another significant area of advancement is in precision psychiatry, which seeks to tailor treatment strategies to individual genetic profiles, brain imaging findings, and psychosocial factors. This approach represents a shift from one-size-fits-all models towards more nuanced understandings of mental illness that can inform targeted interventions. Research into biomarkers and neuroimaging is providing unprecedented detail about the biological underpinnings of mental disorders, promising more effective and personalized treatment plans.

Collaborative networks across disciplines are also enhancing research quality and impact. Partnerships between psychiatrists, psychologists, neuroscientists, and data scientists foster a holistic view of mental health that encompasses biological, psychological, and social dimensions. Such collaborations are crucial for developing comprehensive treatment models that address the multifaceted needs of patients.

Innovations in psychotherapy research are equally noteworthy. The exploration of novel therapeutic approaches such as mindfulness-based stress reduction (MBSR), acceptance and commitment therapy (ACT), and dialectical behavior therapy (DBT) reflects an ongoing commitment to expanding the toolkit for treating anxiety and depression. These modalities emphasize resilience-building, emotional regulation, and behavioral change as key components of recovery.

Finally, patient-centered research methodologies are gaining prominence as essential for understanding the lived experiences of those with mental health conditions. Engaging patients as active participants in research not only enriches study designs but also ensures that outcomes are relevant to those most affected by these illnesses.

In conclusion, research excellence in mental health treatments is characterized by its innovative approaches to understanding and addressing mental illness. By leveraging technology, personalizing care through precision psychiatry, fostering interdisciplinary collaboration, exploring new therapeutic modalities, and prioritizing patient-centered methods, this field continues to advance towards more effective interventions that can significantly improve quality of life for individuals facing mental health challenges.

7.3 The Role of Medication in Treatment Plans

The integration of medication into treatment plans for mental health conditions is a critical component that complements psychotherapeutic interventions, offering a holistic approach to patient care. This section explores the nuanced role of pharmacotherapy in managing mental disorders, emphasizing its importance in conjunction with other treatment modalities.

Medications, including antidepressants, antipsychotics, mood stabilizers, and anxiolytics, play a pivotal role in correcting chemical imbalances in the brain that contribute to mental health conditions. Their use is often essential in reducing symptoms to a manageable level, thereby enhancing the effectiveness of psychotherapy. For many patients, medication can provide significant relief from symptoms that might otherwise hinder their ability to engage fully in therapy.

However, the decision to use medication is highly individualized, taking into account factors such as the severity of symptoms, potential side effects, and patient preferences. It's crucial for healthcare providers to work closely with patients to tailor treatment plans that address their specific needs and concerns. This collaborative approach ensures that medication is used appropriately and effectively as part of a comprehensive treatment strategy.

In recent years, there has been growing interest in precision medicine within psychiatry—tailoring medication choices based on genetic markers or other biomarkers that predict how individuals will respond to specific drugs. This emerging field holds promise for minimizing trial-and-error approaches to finding effective medications and reducing the likelihood of adverse effects.

Moreover, ongoing research into novel pharmacological treatments continues to expand the options available for managing mental health conditions. Breakthroughs such as the approval of esketamine nasal spray for treatment-resistant depression exemplify how innovation in medication development can offer new hope for patients who have not benefited from traditional treatments.

In conclusion, while medications are not a standalone solution for mental health conditions, they are an integral part of comprehensive treatment plans. By alleviating symptoms and stabilizing mood disorders, medications can significantly improve quality of life and facilitate engagement with psychotherapy and other therapeutic interventions. As research advances our understanding of mental illness and treatment responses, personalized approaches to medication management will become increasingly important in optimizing outcomes for individuals with mental health challenges.

8 Customizable Tools for Individual Need

8.1 Adapting Strategies for Personal Circumstances

The journey towards overcoming anxiety and depression is profoundly personal, with each individual facing unique challenges and requiring tailored approaches to manage their mental health effectively. Recognizing the diversity of experiences and needs among those battling these conditions, it becomes crucial to adapt strategies that align with personal circumstances. This adaptation not only enhances the effectiveness of therapeutic interventions but also empowers individuals by acknowledging their autonomy in the healing process.

Personal circumstances can vary widely, encompassing factors such as lifestyle, work environment, social support systems, physical health conditions, and personal preferences. For instance, someone with a demanding job might find brief mindfulness exercises during breaks more feasible than longer meditation sessions. Similarly, individuals with strong social networks may benefit from group therapy or support groups, whereas others might prefer one-on-one counseling or online therapy platforms for privacy reasons.

Moreover, adapting strategies for personal circumstances also involves recognizing and respecting cultural differences in understanding and treating mental health issues. What works in one cultural context may not be applicable or acceptable in another. Therefore, culturally sensitive approaches that respect an individual's background and beliefs are essential for effective intervention.

Identifying personal triggers and stressors to tailor coping mechanisms accordingly.

Adjusting therapeutic techniques to match an individual's learning style (e.g., visual vs. auditory learners).

Incorporating hobbies or interests into therapy to increase engagement (e.g., art therapy for creative individuals).

In conclusion, adapting strategies to fit personal circumstances is not just about modifying techniques; it's about embracing a holistic view of healing that considers all aspects of an individual's life. By doing so, "Breaking Free" underscores the importance of personalized care in the journey towards mental well-being. It encourages readers to actively participate in crafting their path to recovery, ensuring that the strategies they adopt are as unique as their stories.

8.2 Creating Your Mental Health Toolkit

In the journey of managing and overcoming mental health challenges, the creation of a personalized mental health toolkit stands as a cornerstone strategy. This toolkit comprises various coping mechanisms, therapeutic techniques, and self-care practices tailored to meet the unique needs and preferences of an individual. The essence of crafting such a toolkit lies in its ability to offer immediate, accessible support during times of distress or when navigating daily stressors.

The process begins with a deep understanding of one's personal triggers and stressors. Identifying these elements allows for the selection of tools that can effectively mitigate their impact. For instance, someone who finds social interactions draining may include strategies for setting healthy boundaries or techniques for gradual exposure to social settings.

Another critical aspect is incorporating activities that promote relaxation and well-being. This could range from mindfulness exercises, such as meditation or deep-breathing techniques, to physical activities like yoga or walking. The inclusion of hobbies that bring joy and fulfillment also plays a significant role in enhancing one's mental health toolkit. Whether it's painting, reading, or gardening, these activities offer therapeutic benefits by reducing anxiety and improving mood.

Technology offers additional resources for building an effective mental health toolkit. Various apps provide guided meditations, mood tracking features, and cognitive behavioral therapy (CBT) exercises. These digital tools can complement traditional coping strategies by offering on-the-go support and helping individuals stay connected with their progress.

Lastly, the importance of seeking professional guidance cannot be overstated. A therapist or counselor can assist in identifying effective strategies and tools based on an individual's specific circumstances. They can also introduce new techniques that might not have been considered previously, further enriching the mental health toolkit.

In conclusion, creating a personalized mental health toolkit is an empowering step towards managing one's mental well-being. By carefully selecting tools that resonate with personal experiences and preferences, individuals can navigate their mental health journey with greater confidence and resilience.

8.3 Prioritizing Self-Care in Daily Life

In the context of enhancing mental well-being, prioritizing self-care in daily life emerges as a pivotal strategy. This approach not only complements the personalized mental health toolkit discussed previously but also serves as its foundational element. Embracing self-care involves recognizing and addressing one's needs at various levels—physical, emotional, and psychological—to maintain balance and foster resilience against stressors.

The concept of self-care is broad and multifaceted, encompassing a range of practices that nurture the body and mind. It begins with basic yet essential activities such as ensuring adequate sleep, maintaining a nutritious diet, and engaging in regular physical exercise. These fundamental practices lay the groundwork for physical health, which is intrinsically linked to mental well-being.

Beyond physical health, emotional self-care plays a crucial role. This includes developing healthy coping mechanisms for stress, such as journaling, engaging in creative outlets like art or music, and practicing mindfulness techniques. Mindfulness exercises, including meditation and deep breathing, help center thoughts and emotions, providing clarity and calmness in moments of turmoil.

Another dimension of self-care involves social connections. Building and sustaining meaningful relationships contribute significantly to emotional support systems. Whether it's spending time with loved ones or participating in community activities, these interactions can offer solace and joy amidst life's challenges.

Moreover, setting boundaries is an integral aspect of self-care that often goes overlooked. Recognizing limits regarding workloads, social engagements, and even personal interactions helps prevent burnout and ensures that one's own needs are not neglected. Learning to say no is a powerful tool in safeguarding mental health.

In conclusion, integrating self-care into daily living is not merely an act of indulgence but a necessity for sustaining mental health. By adopting practices that promote physical well-being, emotional balance, social connectivity, and personal boundaries, individuals can build resilience against stressors while navigating their journey toward mental wellness with greater confidence.

Ensuring adequate restorative sleep

Maintaining balanced nutrition

Incorporating physical activity into daily routines

Engaging in hobbies or activities that bring joy

Practicing mindfulness to enhance emotional regulation

Cultivating supportive social networks

Setting healthy boundaries across all areas of life

Empirical Evidence and Empathetic Storytelling

9.1 Bridging Science with Human Experience

The intersection of scientific understanding and human experience is a critical frontier in the battle against anxiety and depression. This convergence is not merely about applying theoretical knowledge; it's about transforming that knowledge into a beacon of hope for those ensnared by these conditions. The essence of bridging science with human experience lies in translating empirical evidence into relatable, empathetic narratives that resonate on a personal level.

Scientific research provides us with the tools to understand the biochemical and neurological underpinnings of anxiety and depression. It offers insights into how these conditions affect the brain's structure and function, shedding light on why they manifest in the ways that they do. However, this information alone can feel cold and detached without being woven into the fabric of human stories. By integrating scientific findings with personal accounts, we create a powerful narrative that speaks to both the mind and the heart.

One way this bridge is constructed is through empathetic storytelling, which involves sharing experiences from individuals who have lived through the challenges of anxiety and depression. These stories serve multiple purposes: they validate others' feelings, offer hope, illuminate paths to healing that are grounded in science yet personalized in approach, and demystify these conditions by showing their impact on real lives. Empathetic storytelling acts as a mirror reflecting both shared pain and shared resilience, making the scientific aspects more accessible and relatable.

In addition to personal narratives, practical strategies for managing symptoms are crucial in this bridging effort. Techniques such as cognitive-behavioral therapy (CBT), mindfulness practices, and other therapeutic approaches are presented not just as clinical recommendations but as tools that have been effectively utilized by individuals in their journey toward wellness. Each strategy is backed by scientific research but is also accompanied by firsthand accounts of how these methods can be implemented in daily life.

This holistic approach—melding rigorous science with deeply human stories—empowers readers to see beyond their condition. It fosters a sense of agency by providing them with a comprehensive understanding of what they are facing while simultaneously offering concrete steps for overcoming it. Through this blend of empirical evidence and empathetic storytelling, "Breaking Free" does more than inform; it inspires action, encourages reflection, and builds a community around shared experiences of struggle and triumph.

9.2 Engaging Readers in a Transformative Process

The journey from understanding to transformation is a pivotal aspect of engaging readers, especially when addressing complex issues like anxiety and depression. This process involves not just reading about scientific facts or personal stories but internalizing this information to foster change within oneself. Engaging readers in a transformative process requires a delicate balance between presenting empirical evidence and crafting empathetic narratives that resonate on a deeply personal level.

At the core of this engagement is the concept of active participation. Readers are not passive recipients of information; rather, they are invited to become co-navigators in their journey towards healing and understanding. This participatory approach encourages individuals to reflect on their own experiences, compare them with the stories and data presented, and consider how new strategies could be applied in their lives.

Empathy plays a crucial role in this transformative process. By sharing stories that echo the readers' struggles, fears, and hopes, authors can create a sense of companionship and understanding that transcends the pages of their work. These narratives act as catalysts for change by providing both inspiration and practical examples of overcoming challenges through resilience and determination.

Moreover, integrating interactive elements such as reflective questions, exercises for mental health practices, or prompts for journaling can further enhance engagement. These tools invite readers to actively apply what they have learned, facilitating a deeper connection with the material. It's an approach that not only educates but also empowers readers to take actionable steps towards improving their mental health.

In conclusion, engaging readers in a transformative process is about more than just conveying information; it's about inspiring action and reflection through a combination of scientific insights and empathetic storytelling. By fostering an environment where readers feel seen, understood, and motivated to embark on a path of self-discovery and healing, authors can contribute significantly to their audience's journey towards wellness.

9.3 The Power of Vulnerability in Healing

The concept of vulnerability often carries a negative connotation, suggesting weakness or susceptibility to harm. However, within the context of healing—particularly emotional and psychological healing—vulnerability emerges as a potent force for transformation and growth. Embracing one's vulnerabilities not only fosters self-awareness but also cultivates empathy and connection with others, serving as a cornerstone in the journey towards wellness.

Vulnerability acts as a bridge between empirical evidence and empathetic storytelling, allowing individuals to see their own struggles mirrored in the experiences of others. This reflection is not merely about shared suffering but about recognizing the universal human capacity for resilience and recovery. By opening up about fears, failures, and uncertainties, storytellers invite their audience into a space where healing is seen as both possible and permissible.

This openness can significantly alter the therapeutic process. For practitioners and patients alike, acknowledging vulnerability facilitates a deeper level of trust and communication. It dismantles barriers that often hinder effective treatment—such as stigma or denial—and encourages a more holistic approach to mental health care. In this environment, individuals are more likely to engage with difficult emotions, confront traumatic memories, and experiment with new coping strategies.

Moreover, the power of vulnerability extends beyond individual healing to influence communities and societies at large. When public figures or groups share their vulnerabilities openly, it can challenge societal norms around strength and stoicism, paving the way for more inclusive discussions about mental health. Such shifts are crucial for developing support systems that recognize the complexity of human emotion and prioritize empathy over judgment.

In conclusion, embracing vulnerability in healing processes is transformative. It not only enhances personal growth but also strengthens communal bonds by fostering environments where people feel safe to share their stories without fear of rejection or ridicule. Through this openness, we can collectively move towards a more compassionate understanding of mental health challenges—a critical step in addressing them effectively.

10 Reflective Exercises for Self-Discovery

10.1 Encouraging Active Engagement with Content

In the journey of overcoming anxiety and depression, active engagement with therapeutic content is not just beneficial; it's essential. "Breaking Free: How to Overcome Anxiety and Depression" underscores this by integrating reflective exercises designed to foster a deep, personal connection with the material presented. This approach is rooted in the understanding that healing begins when individuals not only consume information but also interact with it in a way that resonates with their unique experiences and challenges.

The concept of active engagement goes beyond passive reading or listening. It involves a dynamic process where readers are encouraged to reflect on their thoughts, feelings, and behaviors in relation to what they learn from the book. This method serves multiple purposes: it enhances comprehension, facilitates personalization of strategies for managing symptoms, and empowers readers to take actionable steps towards recovery.

One of the key strategies employed in "Breaking Free" to encourage active engagement is the inclusion of guided reflection questions at the end of each chapter. These questions are carefully crafted to prompt introspection and self-discovery, guiding readers through an exploration of how the content specifically applies to their lives. For instance, after discussing cognitive-behavioral techniques for managing anxiety, a reflection question might ask readers to identify specific thought patterns that contribute to their anxious feelings and consider how these might be challenged or reframed.

Another tool for fostering active engagement is the use of personal stories from individuals who have successfully navigated the path out of anxiety and depression. These narratives not only offer hope but also serve as practical examples of how theoretical concepts can be applied in real-life situations.

Readers are encouraged to draw parallels between these stories and their own experiences, thereby making the content more relatable and actionable.

Moreover, "Breaking Free" incorporates interactive elements such as worksheets and checklists that readers can use to apply what they've learned directly into their daily routines. These tools provide a structured framework for practicing new skills, tracking progress over time, and identifying areas that may require additional focus or adjustment.

In conclusion, by encouraging active engagement with its content through reflective exercises, personal stories, and interactive tools, "Breaking Free" does more than just impart knowledge—it invites readers into an immersive process of learning and growth that is both deeply personal and profoundly transformative.

10.2 Fostering Agency in the Healing Journey

The concept of fostering agency plays a pivotal role in the healing journey from anxiety and depression. It involves empowering individuals to take control of their recovery process, making decisions that align with their personal values and goals. This empowerment is crucial because it shifts the perspective from being a passive recipient of care to an active participant in one's own healing. By fostering agency, individuals are encouraged to explore and identify what works best for them, tailoring strategies and interventions to fit their unique needs.

One effective way to foster agency is through setting personal goals related to recovery. These goals provide direction and motivation, serving as benchmarks for progress. For instance, someone might set a goal to practice mindfulness meditation for five minutes each day or to challenge a negative thought pattern each week. Achieving these small but significant milestones can boost confidence and reinforce the individual's ability to influence their own mental health positively.

Another aspect of fostering agency involves informed decision-making about treatment options. This requires access to comprehensive information about different therapeutic approaches, medications, and lifestyle changes that could support recovery. Equipped with knowledge, individuals can engage in meaningful discussions with healthcare providers about the pros and cons of various options, making choices that resonate with their preferences and life circumstances.

Self-monitoring tools such as journals or apps can also enhance agency by allowing individuals to track their symptoms, identify triggers, and notice patterns over time. This self-awareness facilitates a deeper understanding of one's mental health condition and how it interacts with daily activities, thoughts, and feelings. Armed with this insight, individuals can make more informed decisions about managing their condition.

In conclusion, fostering agency in the healing journey is not just about encouraging active participation; it's about nurturing a sense of ownership over one's recovery process. By setting personal goals, making informed decisions about treatment options, and utilizing self-monitoring tools for greater self-awareness, individuals can become empowered agents of their own healing. This empowerment not only supports more personalized and effective management of anxiety and depression but also contributes to a more resilient sense of self.

10.3 Uncovering Personal Strengths and Resilience

In the journey of self-discovery, uncovering personal strengths and resilience stands as a cornerstone for building a fulfilling life. This process not only aids in navigating through challenges but also in harnessing an individual's innate potential for growth and happiness. Understanding one's unique strengths and resilient traits is akin to laying a foundation upon which personal development and achievements can be built.

Identifying personal strengths begins with introspection and reflection. It involves looking back at past experiences, recognizing moments of success, and understanding the qualities that led to those achievements. Whether it's perseverance, creativity, empathy, or leadership, acknowledging these attributes can empower individuals to leverage them more effectively in future endeavors.

Resilience, on the other hand, is about understanding and appreciating one's capacity to recover from difficulties. It's the ability to bounce back from setbacks with greater wisdom and strength. Developing resilience involves adopting a positive mindset, practicing self-compassion, and viewing challenges as opportunities for growth. By reflecting on how they've overcome past hardships, individuals can uncover their resilient nature.

To facilitate this discovery process, engaging in reflective exercises such as journaling or mindfulness practices can be incredibly beneficial. These activities encourage deeper self-exploration by prompting individuals to consider questions like "What am I naturally good at?" or "How have I managed to persevere in tough times?". Such inquiries not only highlight personal strengths but also resilience strategies that have been effective.

Another powerful approach is seeking feedback from friends, family members, or mentors who can offer an external perspective on one's abilities and coping mechanisms. Sometimes others can see aspects of our character that we overlook or undervalue.

In conclusion, uncovering personal strengths and resilience is a transformative process that fosters self-awareness and confidence. By embracing this journey of self-discovery, individuals equip themselves with the knowledge to navigate life's ups and downs more skillfully. Emphasizing these aspects of oneself not only contributes to personal well-being but also enhances one's ability to contribute positively to the lives of others.

11 Navigating Complexities with Confidence

11.1 Overcoming Obstacles in Mental Health Challenges

The journey to overcoming obstacles in mental health challenges is both personal and universal. In the context of increasing rates of anxiety and depression, understanding the multifaceted barriers individuals face is crucial for fostering resilience and promoting recovery. This exploration delves into the complexities surrounding mental health issues, offering insights into navigating these hurdles with confidence.

One significant obstacle is the stigma associated with mental health disorders. Despite growing awareness, societal perceptions can still render individuals reluctant to seek help or share their experiences. The fear of judgment or misunderstanding by peers, family, and even professionals can exacerbate feelings of isolation and despair. Addressing this requires a collective effort to normalize conversations about mental health, emphasizing that seeking support is not only courageous but a critical step towards healing.

Another challenge lies in accessing quality mental health care. Factors such as geographical location, financial constraints, and limited availability of specialized services can hinder individuals from receiving the help they need. Innovative solutions like teletherapy have begun to bridge this gap, offering remote support that transcends traditional barriers. Additionally, community-based initiatives and sliding scale payment options are emerging as vital resources for making mental health care more inclusive and accessible.

Finally, the role of support systems cannot be overstated. Whether through friends, family, or support groups, having a network of understanding individuals provides a foundation of encouragement and empathy essential for navigating the path to wellness. It underscores the notion that no one should have to face these challenges alone.

The internal battle with one's own mind presents perhaps the most personal obstacle. The nature of anxiety and depression can lead to a debilitating cycle of negative self-talk and hopelessness, making it difficult to take the first steps towards recovery. Herein lies the importance of self-compassion and resilience-building strategies. Techniques such as cognitive-behavioral therapy (CBT), mindfulness practices, and physical activity have shown promise in breaking this cycle, empowering individuals to challenge distorted thinking patterns and engage in positive self-care.

In conclusion, overcoming obstacles in mental health challenges demands a multifaceted approach that addresses societal stigma, enhances access to care, combats internal struggles with compassion and resilience strategies, and fosters strong support networks. By acknowledging these hurdles openly and working collectively towards solutions, we pave the way for more people to navigate their mental health journeys with confidence.

11.2 Strategies for Sustaining Progress

In the journey of overcoming mental health challenges, sustaining progress is as crucial as initiating the healing process. This section delves into strategies that not only support continued growth but also help in preventing relapse into old patterns. The essence of these strategies lies in their ability to foster resilience, encourage adaptability, and maintain the momentum of recovery.

The first strategy involves setting realistic and achievable goals. Goals act as milestones that can provide direction and a sense of purpose. However, it's essential that these goals are tailored to an individual's current capabilities and circumstances to avoid feelings of overwhelm or failure. Incremental goals allow for small victories, which can significantly boost confidence and motivation.

Another vital strategy is developing a robust support network. As highlighted previously, the role of supportive relationships cannot be overstated in the realm of mental health recovery. Engaging with friends, family, or support groups who understand your journey can provide a safety net during challenging times. These networks offer emotional sustenance, practical advice, and sometimes just a listening ear when needed.

Maintaining healthy routines plays a pivotal role in sustaining progress. Regular physical activity, balanced nutrition, adequate sleep, and mindfulness practices like meditation can reinforce mental well-being by reducing stress levels and improving overall physical health. These routines become the bedrock upon which long-term recovery is built.

Continuous learning and adaptation form another cornerstone strategy for sustained progress. As individuals evolve through their recovery journey, so too should their coping mechanisms and strategies for dealing with stressors or triggers. This might involve regular sessions with a therapist to refine techniques learned during treatment or exploring new activities that contribute to well-being.

Lastly, embracing self-compassion is fundamental in sustaining mental health progress. Recovery is often non-linear; setbacks may occur. During such times, practicing self-compassion—treating oneself with kindness rather than criticism—can prevent spiraling back into negative thought patterns.

In conclusion, sustaining progress in overcoming mental health challenges requires a multifaceted approach that includes setting achievable goals, building strong support networks, maintaining healthy routines, continuously adapting coping strategies, and practicing self-compassion. By integrating these strategies into daily life, individuals can navigate their recovery journey with greater resilience and confidence.

11.3 Building Resilience in the Face of Adversity

Building resilience is a critical aspect of navigating through life's inevitable challenges and adversities. It involves developing the mental and emotional toughness to cope with stress, overcome obstacles, and bounce back from setbacks stronger than before. This section explores the multifaceted approach to fostering resilience, offering insights into how individuals can cultivate this invaluable trait within themselves.

Resilience is not an innate quality but a skill that can be developed over time through intentional practice and mindset shifts. One of the foundational steps in building resilience is recognizing and accepting that adversity is a part of life. This acceptance does not mean resignation but rather acknowledging challenges without letting them define or overwhelm you.

Maintaining a positive outlook is another crucial element in developing resilience. Optimism doesn't ignore reality but chooses to focus on what can be controlled and finding lessons even in difficult situations. Cultivating gratitude by regularly reflecting on what you are thankful for can significantly shift perspective, making it easier to see the positives amidst adversity.

Self-awareness plays a pivotal role in resilience-building as well. Understanding your thoughts, emotions, and reactions helps in identifying patterns that may exacerbate stress or hinder recovery. Through self-reflection, individuals can learn to adapt their responses to challenges, adopting more constructive coping mechanisms over time.

Another key strategy is leveraging support networks. Connection with others provides emotional sustenance, practical assistance, and a sense of belonging—all essential components for weathering tough times. Engaging with friends, family members, mentors, or professional support services can offer new viewpoints and solutions while reinforcing the idea that you're not alone in your struggles.

Finally, embracing change as an opportunity for growth is integral to building resilience. Adversity often forces us out of our comfort zones but also presents chances for personal development and discovering strengths we may not have realized we possessed. By viewing challenges as catalysts for learning and transformation, individuals can navigate life's ups and downs with greater ease and confidence.

In conclusion, building resilience in the face of adversity requires a combination of acceptance, optimism, self-awareness, support systems, and seeing change as an opportunity for growth. By integrating these strategies into daily life practices, individuals equip themselves with the tools necessary to face hardships head-on and emerge stronger on the other side.

Pathway Illuminated by Compassion and Practical W

12.1 Supporting Others in Their Battle Against Anxiety and Depression

In the journey to support others as they confront anxiety and depression, understanding the multifaceted nature of these conditions is paramount. This endeavor not only requires empathy and patience but also a strategic approach that combines knowledge with actionable support mechanisms. The significance of this support system cannot be understated, as it provides a lifeline to those who are navigating through their darkest times.

The first step in offering meaningful assistance is to educate oneself about the symptoms, triggers, and underlying causes of anxiety and depression. This knowledge equips supporters with the ability to recognize signs of distress and understand the complexities involved in these mental health challenges. It's crucial to approach conversations with sensitivity and openness, creating a safe space for individuals to share their experiences without fear of judgment.

Listening plays a critical role in providing support. It involves more than just hearing words; it's about validating feelings, acknowledging struggles, and showing genuine concern. Active listening can help individuals feel seen and understood, which is incredibly powerful when they're feeling isolated by their condition.

Beyond these actions, it's important to maintain consistency in your support. Check-in regularly with your loved one, offer reminders of their strengths and progress, and celebrate small victories together. Remember that recovery from anxiety and depression is a journey with ups and downs; your unwavering presence can make all the difference.

Encourage professional help: Gently suggest seeking advice from mental health professionals when appropriate. Offer assistance in finding resources or making appointments if needed.

Support through lifestyle changes: Encourage participation in activities known to improve mental health, such as exercise, healthy eating, and adequate sleep. Offer to join them in these activities as a form of solidarity.

Stay informed: Keep abreast of new treatments, therapies, and support groups that could benefit your loved one. Information is empowering both for you and for them.

In conclusion, supporting someone battling anxiety or depression demands compassion coupled with practical wisdom. By educating yourself on these conditions, actively listening with empathy, encouraging professional help when necessary, supporting healthy lifestyle changes, staying informed about new developments in mental health care, and being consistently present—you become an invaluable ally in their healing process.

12.2 Conclusion: Reclaiming Control Over Mental Well-being

The journey towards reclaiming control over one's mental well-being is both profound and personal. It transcends the mere act of managing symptoms; it involves a holistic reevaluation of how we perceive, engage with, and ultimately support our mental health. This concluding section delves into the essence of taking proactive steps towards mental wellness, emphasizing the power of individual agency coupled with community support.

Understanding that mental well-being is not a static state but a dynamic process is crucial. It requires continuous effort and adaptation to life's ever-changing circumstances. Empowerment in this context means recognizing when to seek help, when to apply self-care strategies, and when to lean on the strength of community and relationships. The path to improved mental health is paved with knowledge, self-awareness, and the courage to face challenges head-on.

One pivotal aspect of reclaiming control over mental well-being is education. By educating ourselves about the nature of mental health conditions, their triggers, and effective coping mechanisms, we demystify these experiences and reduce stigma. Knowledge empowers individuals to make informed decisions about their care and fosters a sense of autonomy in managing their health.

Developing resilience through mindfulness practices such as meditation or yoga can enhance one's ability to cope with stress and anxiety.

Building a supportive network that includes friends, family, healthcare providers, and peer support groups creates a safety net that can catch us during times of need.

Adopting healthy lifestyle habits—such as regular physical activity, balanced nutrition, adequate sleep, and abstaining from substance abuse—lays a foundation for both physical and mental health.

In conclusion, reclaiming control over mental well-being is an empowering journey that blends self-care with external support. It involves making conscious choices every day that prioritize our health and happiness. By fostering resilience, seeking knowledge, building supportive networks, and embracing healthy lifestyles, we can navigate the complexities of mental health with confidence and compassion. Remembering that this journey is unique for each individual encourages patience and understanding both for ourselves and others as we walk this path together.

12.3 Embracing a Brighter Future with Hope and Confidence

The journey towards a brighter future, filled with hope and confidence, is an essential continuation of the process of reclaiming control over mental well-being. This pathway is not just about overcoming present challenges but also about envisioning and moving towards a future where mental health is nurtured and protected. Embracing this future requires a blend of optimism, practical strategies, and the belief that change is possible and within reach.

Hope plays a pivotal role in this journey. It acts as the light that guides individuals through dark times, offering a sense of possibility that things can improve. Hope is more than wishful thinking; it's grounded in the belief that our actions can lead to positive outcomes. Cultivating hope involves setting achievable goals, recognizing small victories, and appreciating the progress made on the path to wellness.

Confidence in one's ability to face future challenges grows from past successes and learned resilience. Building confidence means acknowledging one's strengths, learning from setbacks without being defined by them, and understanding that every step forward contributes to personal growth. It involves trusting oneself to navigate uncertainty and make decisions that support mental health.

To embrace a brighter future with hope and confidence, several strategies can be employed:

Continuously setting realistic goals that motivate action and provide direction.

Maintaining an attitude of gratitude by recognizing and appreciating what is good in life, even during tough times.

Seeking out stories of resilience that inspire and remind us of the strength of the human spirit to overcome adversity.

Investing in relationships that provide support, understanding, and encouragement.

Staying informed about mental health resources and tools that can aid in navigating future challenges more effectively.

In conclusion, embracing a brighter future with hope and confidence is an integral part of sustaining mental well-being. It requires an ongoing commitment to self-care, learning, growth, and connection with others. By fostering hope and building confidence in our ability to face whatever lies ahead, we open ourselves up to endless possibilities for happiness and fulfillment. This proactive stance empowers individuals not only to dream of a better tomorrow but also to take concrete steps towards making it a reality.

"Breaking Free: How to Overcome Anxiety and Depression" is a pivotal nonfiction book addressing the escalating prevalence of anxiety and depression in today's society. With nearly 264 million people globally affected by depression, and a significant portion also grappling with anxiety disorders, the book serves as an essential guide for individuals facing these mental health challenges, their supporters, and anyone interested in mental health awareness. It aims to empower readers with knowledge, strategies, and hope for overcoming these conditions.

The book begins by exploring the multifaceted nature of anxiety and depression, providing readers with a deep understanding of these conditions beyond basic definitions. It covers their physiological, psychological, and social aspects, incorporating recent research findings to make complex scientific concepts accessible. Personal stories from those who have battled anxiety and depression offer real-life insights into the struggles and victories over these invisible adversaries, validating readers' experiences and highlighting diverse healing journeys.

Following this foundation, "Breaking Free" presents practical strategies for managing symptoms and building resilience. It introduces a range of therapeutic approaches including cognitive-behavioral techniques and mindfulness practices, complemented by expert opinions to ensure reliability. The book emphasizes customization of tools to fit individual needs, acknowledging the uniqueness of each person's journey towards mental well-being.

By combining empirical evidence with empathetic storytelling and reflective exercises, "Breaking Free" not only educates but also engages readers in a transformative process towards regaining control over their mental health. This comprehensive guide encourages active participation in one's healing journey, offering a pathway illuminated by compassion, insight, and practical wisdom for navigating mental health challenges.

www.ingramcontent.com/pod-product-compliance
Lightning Source LLC
Chambersburg PA
CBHW072000210526
45479CB00003B/1008